FRAZIER PUBLISHING and SERVICES
P.O. Box 363835
North Las Vegas, NV 89036-7835

Disclaimer: This book is sold with the understanding that the author and publisher are not engaged in offering legal advice. The purpose of this book is to complement and supplement other text on the subject. You are urged to read all available information and learn as much as possible before starting. Every effort has been made to make this book as accurate as possible. Use this book as a general guide and be sure to check the laws and regulations in your area before starting. The author shall have no liability and responsibility to any person or entity, with respect to the loss or damage caused, or alleged to be caused, directly or indirectly by the information contained in this book. This book is not affiliated with any government.

Contents

Did you know some tenants who take customer service way too far! A tenant is a customer. You, the property owner provide a service, the service of room and board. There are tenants that will nitpick over every little thing and never pay their rent late. The unnecessary complaints are many.

These tenants are like restaurant customers who consume half their meal, then complain to the food server about their meal and refuse to pay for the meal. Nine times out of ten your splinter in the foot tenant may have an issue and may be violating their rental agreement with you. Do your homework as you explore, "How to Keep Good Tenants and Evict Bad Ones"

Don't Discriminate

Federal Anti-Discrimination Law

Federal law prohibits discrimination on the following basis:

Race

Color

Religion

National origin,

Sex

Age

Family status

(Including not allowing children, discrimination against pregnant women)

Physical disability

Mental disability
(Including alcoholism and past drug addiction)

Cities and States have various housing laws, and yours may prohibit other kinds of discrimination, or discriminatory conduct such as:

Marital status

Sexual orientation

Here are 8 additional Federal Anti-Discrimination Laws:

1. Advertising cannot contain any statement indicating a preference or limitation based on any of the protected classes listed above.

2. The landlord may not make any similar implication or statement.

3. A landlord cannot say that an apartment is not available when in fact it is available.

4. A landlord cannot use a different set of rules for assessing applicants belonging to a protected class.

5. A landlord cannot refuse to rent to persons in a protected class.

6. A landlord cannot provide different services or facilities to tenants in a protected class or require a larger deposit, or treat late rental payments differently.

7. A landlord cannot end a tenancy for a discriminatory reason.

8. A landlord cannot harass a tenant.

Service Animals

A landlord cannot refuse to rent to someone because of a "no pets" policy if a person has trained a helper animal, such as a seeing-eye dog, or a dog that helps them negotiate with a physical or mental disability. If the landlord does refuse, he or she has violated federal law, including the Americans with Disabilities Act.

Example: A jury in Minneapolis, Minnesota, recently awarded large damages to a man who was grief-stricken after his son murder and had begun taking care of his son's dog at the suggestion of his therapist. Before he started taking care of the dog he was severely depressed and not functioning normally. The jury concluded that enforcing the landlord's no-pets policy under those circumstances was a form of disability discrimination.

Disclosure Requirements

If a landlord rejected someone because they received negative information from previous landlords, employers, other third parties or bank, the rejected potential tenant has a right to know why.

Under the federal Fair Credit Reporting Act a landlord has to tell individuals if their rejection was based on negative credit information that came from a source other than their credit report.

The Federal Fair Credit Reporting Act also requires a landlord to tell an individual that they were rejected due to negative credit information.

After receiving your request for disclosure of the negative information, the landlord must tell you "the nature of the information," within a "reasonable time." The law does not indicate how much detail the landlord must give someone.

Right to a Habitable Home
Tenants have the right to live in "habitable" premises. The following conditions could make premises "uninhabitable."

Unsafe conditions, such as holes in the floor, plaster coming down from the ceiling, bad wiring, and gross infestation of vermin such as cockroaches or mice.

Lead Content
Under federal law, rental housing must be free of lead-based paint. It is more typical in older buildings, and up to 75 percent of the housing stock is still affected by it. No matter how old or new the premises are, watch for chipping paint, peeling paint, flaking paint, and paint dust.

Warning: Lead-based paint is extremely dangerous to small children and pets, causing damage to the central nervous system. Crawling and toddling children interact with their environments by putting things in their mouths, and paint dust is easily inhaled. The consequences for your children could include

Screen the Tenant

It's been said that "95% of your tenant problems can be eliminated in the screening process. Below are 5 Steps a landlord can follow when it comes to screening tenants.

STEP 1: First Contact

From the very first contact with the tenant, the screening process has begun. Whether you are the landlord, real estate agent or property manager, the same still holds true. First Contact is usually by telephone*, so you need to ask the right qualifying questions in order to decide if you should proceed to

STEP 2: Advise

Customers of your upfront rent and security deposit requirements and other important facts regarding the rental that may help disqualify the prospect. I suggest you make a list or prospect card of questions to ask and have it handy while you conduct your first contact interview. For example:

NAME :	PHONE :
REASON FOR MOVING :	# OF PEOPLE & RELATIONSHIP :
INTENDED RENTAL TERM :	OCCUPANCY DATE :
PETS :	SMOKING :
CREDIT :	LANDLORD REFERENCE :

* First contact can also be through an Internet ad by email. This is becoming a more popular method of rental advertising and I have found huge savings in rental advertising money. Here is a link to my Pre-screening Tenant Prospect Card for Internet ads, such as Craigslist or LPA Rental Ads, etc. Pre-screening Tenant Prospect Card.

Please note that anyone who has a problem answering your questions (as long as you ask them politely), probably will not qualify for your rental. Serious customers want to make a good impression on you and should be happy to answer your questions. This process can save you and customers a lot of time and trouble.

STEP 3: Showing the Property
From landlords to real estate agents, we all have our own style in showing the rental. I think we all need to be aware of certain significant signs to watch for while evaluating your prospective new tenants.

1. Appearance. Is the prospect neat and clean? Did he or she make an attempt to make a good impression? In most cases, an unkempt person keeps an unkempt lifestyle and home.

2. Car. Does the prospect have a nice car? Is it clean? Although we can't judge people by their car, we should take note of it along with other details.

3. Attitude & Manners. Does this prospect behave respectfully? Does he or she show indications of being difficult to deal with in the future? Did the prospect wipe his or her feet when stepping into the house? Did the prospect walk into the rental while smoking? You can learn a lot about people even before speaking to them. Sometimes it helps to pay attention to details.

4. Criticizing the property. Are the prospects pointing out legitimate concerns, or are they trying to come up with items to negotiate price?

5. Yes or No? Can the prospect make the decision now or will they have to think about it? If they know now that they want your rental, did the prospect come ready to give you a deposit and fill out an application?

STEP 3: The Application Process
The first thing you need is a quality rental application. Let the applicant know that his or her application will be considered along with others, and you will notify the applicant once a decision is made. Advise the applicant(s) that it is very important to fill out the application as completely as possible. If you (and I recommend you do) run a credit report on the applicant, I suggest you be sure to collect a screening fee if possible. Inform your prospective tenant that the application must be returned as soon as possible to avoid the risk of losing the rental to a competing prospect. Review and verify the application thoroughly and look for inconsistencies and "red

flags". When you are satisfied, you will proceed to approving your new tenant in step 4.

STEP 4: The Approval Process

This is usually a fun part, but keep in mind that you are still screening the applicant while preparing him or her for the next step. I like to congratulate the applicant on being approved and let them know they came in 1st place. Also, let them know if you made any special concessions just for them, such as overlooking minor credit infractions, etc.

This process is also an opportunity for you to make sure the applicant can and will deliver. Set the time, date and place for your lease signing. Instruct the applicant(s) to bring the proper amounts of monies, identification (if you don't already have it), and how you prefer to be paid. (Check*, money order or cash)

* Be sure to tell your new tenants that possession or keys will be given only after checks have cleared.

STEP 5: The Lease Signing

It is very important that you have a quality residential lease. You'll be surprised at how many people would just sign a lease without reading it! And I don't just mean tenants! I believe it is crucial to read the entire lease with the tenants at a lease signing. It is your agreement with them. Shouldn't you both know what is really being agreed to? As you read the terms of the lease with the tenants, you will be able to conduct your

5th and final step of screening. Does the tenant argue on every item? Is the late charge an issue? And so on. Of course, if you are unhappy with how your prospect responds to you and/or your lease, you must not rent to this person. I believe: "It is better to have NO tenant than it is to have the wrong tenant." - John Nuzzolese

Tales of a Tenant

Skipping out on rent
"The absolute worst experience we ever had was two college students referred to us by my husband's uncle. They trashed the place, stopped paying rent after the first two months and were really, really difficult to evict because it was winter, and at that time the state had laws protecting tenants from being pitched out into the cold. The final insult, of course, was that when they did sneak away in the dark of night, they turned off the heat but not the water so we had frozen pipes to deal with on top of the garbage and filth."
 --Cynical2

Stealing from the landlord
"I had three rental properties. Worst case was a very rich guy, family lots of $, lots of $! He had utilities cut off, so he tapped into my property's electrical lines with an extension cord and ran four heaters off it for a month, until it burned through on the new hardwood floor. Then he stripped wallpaper and moldings and sold them at a wood-supply business. He tried to take fixtures but was surprised by another tenant, who called me. He skipped. Family is still very big $ and supports him, I have been told, but they won't pay any back rent or damage costs. I was out $3,700 for him the cost of his mountain bike, he told me once."
--Noroom

"I have a coin-operated laundry in one complex. The tenants try everything to get free laundry. Foreign change, metal objects, latex gloves with the quarter in the finger hole (thought that was creative). After they got tired of trying to get free laundry, they decided to just take the actual dryer! Just loaded it up, carried it off and threw it down a hill. I hope they enjoyed the 10 bucks they got out of it!" -- Norcal Landlord

"We recently bought a new house that was a little out of our league, but being that it was four bedrooms, we figured we could rent out a room for some help with the mortgage, and so we did. We found a tenant who was single, didn't drink, didn't smoke and didn't do drugs. He had a cat but said it would stay in the room (I'm allergic). So we accepted him. Long story short, his cat ran around the house, scratched my dog and the furniture, and he did drink, and he did do drugs. The one thing he never did: pay his rent on time. Oh, yeah, and he was married. One day, his estranged wife came to town with a one-way ticket and moved in with no money and a drug problem. Lo and behold, while we were out working all day, she was snooping around the house . . . "collecting" things. First, the boat hitch was missing, and then my shoes. We logged on to our banking account one day and saw there was a check made out to cash, not in our handwriting (and "dollars" was spelled wrong), with the wife's account number and signature on the back.

Needless to say, we evicted them immediately and discovered she had half my wardrobe, and I am still finding things missing!" -- Tahoe Tessy

Friends and Family
"I had let my cousin at the request of my aunt) move in, and she sold my water heater, air-conditioning unit, all the fixtures in the house and all my children's furniture and living-room furniture I had let her use, my riding lawn mower and anything else she could remove. Then she left in the middle of the night. Now, two years later, she has no problem walking into any family gathering and acting like she does not understand why I do not speak with her." -- Amalga

"I had close relatives (too close) living in my house. One moved out, and a girlfriend moved in. I haven't had any rent money in six months because she is in school, and if I make too much of a fuss they will all be mad at me. This is a no-win situation. I found out not to have dealings with family!!" -- Lizzy221

Letting pets run wild
"I rented to a veterinarian who had her boyfriend move in. The two of them started collecting animals. I had agreed to an outside dog only, but now they had four horses, six dogs, and I couldn't count how many cats! They had fenced in the backyard and put the horses in the yard, right up to the back door, and had the

basement full of animals and couldn't possibly clean up after them. Then she left this guy. He stayed, and the contract was only in her name. We couldn't get this guy out of our home." -- Wahoo1413

"My boss has a rental that I got put in charge of, and I will never do that again! It was an older couple with their 20-something-year-old daughter, and they lived in filth. They had two dogs, one cat and a chicken that all lived in the house. I guess the animals didn't like to go outside, so by the time they finally moved out there were mountains of dog, cat and chicken poop in the house. We ended up having to go to court to get them out and then go to court again to get two months of rent and more of a deposit." -- Mandalou

Beyond normal wear and tear
"We had druggies (highly recommended by family/friends in our church!) who glued pennies to the walls, stuffed cheetos into the shutters, stapled small pieces of cardboard to the inside window facings, disassembled the outdoor flower bed and brought all the bricks inside the house, poured water into the floor furnace, causing it to rust out (we have a 1928 home in Tulsa, Okla., which was beautiful), used the drapery for cleaning rags, used wood staples to anchor a large, outdoor inflatable toy inside the living room and left their drug paraphernalia in the closet when they moved. We've spent thousands in cleaning and replacement costs." -- Taken in Tulsa

"The worst case was a house where the renter had driven his four-wheeler into the carpeted living room and repaired it there. When they moved out, they left garbage, dirty diapers on the carpet, children's drawing in permanent marker on the wall, feces in a plugged toilet, spoiled food in the fridge and, oddly, all sorts of furniture and baby items." -- bulldog7

"I am out of the rental-property business, thank goodness. The worst were the people who paid the first and last months' rent, then moved in and never paid another dime. After repeated calls and personal visits I had to pay $100 to the constable to get them out. After the constable told them to get out, they shattered the solid-core front door, poured paraffin down all the drains, rewired the electric wiring to short out the whole system (so the fireman told me), threw beer bottles and broke all the windows and screens out, and sold all furniture and appliances and some carpet ripped off the floor. What carpet they did not steal, they poured bleach on, and dumped battery acid on the tile flooring. They put knife holes in all the Sheetrock and left me with original spray paintings. The water had been cut off for months, and they were using 3-pound butter tubs for their toilet, which they left me with. Their dogs left presents inside the house, also." -- bothgone

"Rented to a well-to-do couple with a 2-year-old, solid references (so we thought), and we paid a rental agency to monitor the property and collect the rent.

These people paid on time. However, they had a kitchen fire due to the stove being so filthy, thousands of dollars in smoke and fire damage, completely melted the door off the microwave, wouldn't set up the sprinkler-system timers to water automatically, so the entire yard died, completely tore out shrubs and cracked the upstairs master-bath sink washing a bowling ball. They didn't have a diaper pail, so they just tossed the wet diapers (from second child born while in the home) in a corner on the carpet of the baby's room (gag), took every window covering and tore out the alarm system contacts on all the windows. My favorite one: They drove their car through the wall in the garage into the downstairs guest bathroom. All toilets in all three bathrooms had to be replaced because they were stained black. Never could figure that one out." -- Nutso

In a class of their own
"(The tenant) left us with garbage and tons of clothes throughout the house, holes in the walls, carpets destroyed and a large potbellied pig left in the backyard that was very hungry and chased after me." -- Rhonda Landlord

"We fell for a sob story from a prospective tenant, and we got burned. Her husband worked late hours, and she asked if she could take an application with her, (and) along with that could she take the key so they could come by when he got off work at midnight so she could show him the house. She loved the place;

they were going to fill out the application and drop it off to us the next day along with a deposit to hold the property until the credit checks came in. We got a strange call from her a few days later, and on a hunch, my husband and I went by the house. Oh, yes, they were moved in all right; everything was unpacked hanging on the wall, and a cat running around. We had squatters. After the cops were called and the eviction process was started, they had the nerve to ask us if they could start over if they gave us the deposit then." -- it ain't always easy

"I had rented to a mother and two boys (ages 3 and 7) who were supplied to me by the Department of Social Services. They were on a plan (two-year max) to help down-and-out single moms/dads get on their feet. I thought this was a good plan. Then the constant traffic started coming to the house apartment: 10 p.m., 1 p.m., 2:30 p.m., and 6:30 p.m. The smell from the apartment was horrible, and I eventually found out she was making and selling crack cocaine from my apartment." -- Pacific Heights

That's a Good Idea

Evicting a tenant can sometimes be difficult and costly. State and local laws governing evictions vary significantly. It almost takes an act of Congress to evict a tenant in the state California, while in a state like Georgia renter's possessions will be tossed to the street curb in a short period of time. The following tips should help if you if you find yourself in this unfortunate situation.

Hire a Private Detective

A private detective can sit outside your property and wait for the siren in your ear tenant to walk that small dog late at night. The detective can pose as a bum and wait for the cat to look out the window. The detective can also befriend the headache tenant and inform you of all types of violations. Once you have tour solid evidence you can serve them with an eviction. Develop a relationship with a paralegal or a real estate law firm. They can help you with eviction issues and handle legal actions for you.

Make Nice With Your Tenants Neighbors

If you don't like your toothache tenant you can bet your rental income that your tenant has a neighbor or neighbors that feel the same way you do. The neighbor will tell all. The neighbor can inform you if your tenant is using illegal drugs such as marijuana or crystal meth. The neighbor can inform you if your sneaky tenant has someone living with them whom are not on the lease.

Once you have solid evidence from the neighbor such as a written statement of your tenant's violations, proceed with an eviction. Be sure to let the Judge know that you would like to keep the identity of the neighbor private. Give the neighbor gifts on the holidays to show your appreciation but don't ever let the tenants be informed of these gifts.

Raise the Rent

If you have a tenant who rents from you month-to-month, raise the rent. You are within your rights to do so. Raise the rent as high as the law will permit.

Restraining Order

Do you have a bully tenant? Have you ever been threatened by your tenant, if so file a restraining order. This is a very good way to get rid of a harassing tenant.

Visit Your Properties Local Law Enforcement

As the property owner you may able to retrieve a report from the police department regarding rental your property. The local law enforcement may be able to inform you of rental violations you had no knowledge of such as, domestic violence and violent co-inhabitant issues. If there is a situation where the police were called to your property you will find that your unwise decision making tenant's first words to the police were "I let them live with me for a little while. I was trying to help them out. They are not on the lease I want them gone". This is also a possible clause you can use in your leasing agreement.

Retrieve the incident report from the police department and proceed with your eviction.

Eviction Time

An Application for Eviction needs to be issued out of either a High Court or Magistrate's Court asking for the eviction of your tenant. The application contains a short affidavit and the lease agreement.

The application is served upon the Municipality and on your tenant.

Usually your tenant has five business days to oppose the application. In most cases, this isn't done. After the five days has lapsed, an application to the court without giving notice to your Tenant is brought immediately.

The court order and the notice will then be served to your tenant and the jurisdiction.

The court then hears the matter and the eviction order may be granted. The eviction order can order your tenant to be evicted immediately, but "normally it grants the tenant 30 days to vacate the premises. If they fail to do so, the Sheriff of the Court can evict them.

Screen potential tenants efficiently to ensure you don't have to go through an eviction. Please use these procedures to get rid of a 'bad tenant' legally.

www.ingramcontent.com/pod-product-compliance
Lightning Source LLC
Chambersburg PA
CBHW070922210326
41521CB00010B/2282